Original title:
The Courage to Love

Copyright © 2024 Swan Charm
All rights reserved.

Author: Kätriin Kaldaru
ISBN HARDBACK: 978-9916-89-799-7
ISBN PAPERBACK: 978-9916-89-800-0
ISBN EBOOK: 978-9916-89-801-7

The Stone of Hope in Love's Landscape

In the garden where love blooms bright,
The stone of hope stands gleaming white.
With whispers soft, the heart does mend,
A testament to love that will not bend.

Under skies of azure grace,
We find our strength in this sacred space.
With faith as our guide, we journey through,
Believing in the beauty, love will renew.

Amidst the trials that life may bring,
A melody of hope starts to sing.
With every tear that streams down raw,
We rise again, anchored by the law.

A touch of kindness, a glance divine,
In love's embrace, our hearts combine.
The stone of hope, steadfast and true,
In this landscape of love, we start anew.

So let us gather, hand in hand,
As we traverse this blessed land.
With every step in love's great name,
The stone of hope, forever aflame.

Prayers Anchor Us in Love

In quiet whispers, hearts entwine,
Through sacred moments, love's design.
With every prayer, we cast our net,
Anchored in faith, we won't forget.

Through trials faced, we rise anew,
In each embrace, we find the true.
Divine connection, strong and clear,
With every prayer, we draw Him near.

Celestial Bonds, Unbroken

Stars above and hearts below,
In the night, our spirits glow.
Bound by love, we'll never stray,
In celestial light, we find our way.

Threads of faith in heaven's seam,
Together we will chase the dream.
Hand in hand, we navigate,
Celestial bonds, a steadfast fate.

Believers in Love's Miracles

In whispered hopes, we dare to trust,
Each miracle born of love's pure gust.
With open hearts, we seek the light,
Believers true, in faith's delight.

Through every trial, love will prevail,
Guiding us through life's winding trail.
In unity, we rise above,
Together strong, we're lit by love.

Heart Beats with the Divine

In every heartbeat, He resides,
In whispers soft, the Spirit guides.
Through sacred rhythms, life unfolds,
A tapestry of love retold.

In quiet moments or loud refrain,
In joy and sorrow, love remains.
With hearts aligned, we choose the path,
Together bask in His sweet grace.

Celestial Dance of Intimate Souls

In twilight's soft embrace, we glide,
Two spirits intertwined, side by side.
Beneath the stars, our whispers flow,
A sacred rhythm, a gentle glow.

With every heartbeat, the cosmos sways,
Illuminating paths in luminous ways.
Together we flourish, in faith's sweet trance,
In this celestial dance, we find our chance.

The Altar of Shared Breath

Before the flame, we bow our heads,
Binding our hearts, where love is fed.
With shared breath, we ignite the fire,
A union blessed, our souls aspire.

In silence deep, our spirits meet,
The altar glows beneath our feet.
Through trials faced, and burdens shared,
In holy trust, our love declared.

Winged Hearts Freely Given

With open wings, we soar above,
Finding solace in boundless love.
Each flutter whispers a sacred vow,
In tender moments, we live in now.

Freely given, these hearts unite,
Guided by faith, in shared delight.
In every challenge, hand in hand,
Together we rise, a joyful band.

Transparent Hopes Under Sacred Skies

Beneath the dawn's soft, radiant light,
Our hopes emerge, so pure and bright.
With transparent dreams, we reach for grace,
Under sacred skies, we find our place.

In every tear, a lesson learned,
In every joy, our spirits turned.
Together we stand, in love's sweet thrall,
In this holy journey, we embrace it all.

Cherubs Carrying Our Prayers

In the stillness of night,
Cherubs take flight,
Their wings whisper low,
Carrying prayers like snow.

In the heart of the sacred,
Forgiveness cascaded,
Each whisper a song,
Binding us, where we belong.

Through shadows we wander,
In faith, we ponder,
With light ever near,
Our hopes rise sincere.

Under stars that gleam bright,
Guided by holy light,
They dance in the sky,
Our whispered pleas on high.

With each prayer we share,
A celestial flare,
Love's gentle embrace,
Cherubs' grace in this place.

In Love's Embrace, Heavens Open

In the warmth of the morn,
Where new dreams are born,
Heaven's doors gently sway,
Welcoming love's pure ray.

Each heart beats as one,
Underneath the bright sun,
In whispers, we find peace,
In love, our fears cease.

With arms wide to the sky,
We raise our voices high,
In love's sweet refrain,
Our joy, unchained, remains.

All burdens now lighter,
Faith growing ever brighter,
In this embrace divine,
Our spirits align, entwine.

As stars gather above,
We shine with His love,
In heaven's warm glow,
We find strength to grow.

The Flame of Promise on the Sacred Path

On the road that we tread,
Where angels gently spread,
The flame of promise shines,
Through valleys, over pines.

Each step is a vow,
To the sacred now,
With hope as our guide,
In His love, we abide.

Through trials and pain,
In joy or in rain,
The flame will not fade,
In His light, we're remade.

With courage, we sing,
To the heart of the King,
In this moment so clear,
Our truth is sincere.

As the journey unfolds,
With faith we uphold,
The flame fiercely burns,
In the love that returns.

Trust's Temple Built on Souls' Harmony

In trust, our hearts meet,
With rhythm so sweet,
A temple we rise,
Underneath open skies.

Through trials we face,
In His boundless grace,
Each soul intertwined,
In love's light defined.

With every soft prayer,
Our burdens we share,
In laughter, in cries,
Together we rise.

In harmony's song,
We find where we belong,
Each echo resounds,
In peace that surrounds.

This temple, our home,
In unity, we roam,
In trust's gentle fold,
Our spirits turn gold.

Radiant Love Casts Out Shadows

In the dusk of doubt, love's light beams,
Chasing away the shadows, it redeems.
With every heartbeat, grace flows near,
In the embrace of kindness, we persevere.

The veil of despair begins to part,
As radiant love ignites the heart.
In every soul, a spark resides,
Guided by faith, the spirit abides.

Divine Light in the Realm of Souls

In the tapestry of life, bright threads weave,
Divine light beckons, making us believe.
Through trials faced in tempest's roar,
Hope shines through each open door.

Whispers of the heavens soothe the night,
Guiding lost souls towards the light.
In unity we rise, together we stand,
Held in the warmth of a loving hand.

Hymns of Dedication and Hope

With hearts ablaze, we lift our song,
In dedication to the love that's strong.
From valleys deep to mountains high,
We sing our hymns, our spirits fly.

In moments dark, a spark ignites,
Hope is the flame, through endless nights.
Together we journey, side by side,
In faith and trust, our spirits abide.

Fearless Hearts Beneath Divine Wings

Beneath the wings of providence, we soar,
Fearless hearts, together we implore.
Through storms and trials, we find our way,
Guided by love, come what may.

In every challenge, courage will bloom,
With faith as our shield, we conquer gloom.
The bonds we share, unbreakably strong,
In the arms of love, forever we belong.

Heartstrings Plucked by the Infinite

In the stillness of the morn,
Whispers of love gently call,
Threads of grace weave through time,
Hearts awake to the divine.

Each beat echoes holy hymns,
Singing praises to the skies,
Infinite love surrounds us,
In every tear, a blessing lies.

Mountains bow in reverence,
As rivers dance to sacred sound,
Through valleys deep and shadows,
His light in us is found.

With every breath, we surrender,
To the rhythm of His will,
In the tapestry of the cosmos,
We find our spirits filled.

So let your heartstrings tremble,
Plucked by hands of grace,
For in this holy moment,
We discover our true place.

In the Silence, Love Speaks

In the quiet dusk of evening,
Where shadows whisper soft,
Love's essence blooms like flowers,
In the spaces we have sought.

Stillness holds profound secrets,
In the absence of the noise,
Hearts connect in gentle silence,
In the trust of faith, rejoice.

Each heartbeat sings of longing,
Of the bond that will not break,
In the silence, love speaks softly,
A promise we must make.

Though the world may seem to thunder,
And storms rage in the night,
In the heart's hushed sanctuary,
Love illuminates the light.

Let us linger in this moment,
Where time ceases to exist,
In the silence, we find solace,
In His everlasting kiss.

The Sacredness of Letting Go

In the grip of fleeting hours,
We find strength in the release,
Letting go of worldly shadows,
Embracing our soul's peace.

Like autumn leaves that surrender,
To the winds of change that blow,
We trust in the great unfolding,
In the sacredness of letting go.

Each burden lifted gently,
Reveals a path anew,
In every loss, a blessing,
In the heart's sweet venue.

So we breathe and we release,
All chains that hold us tight,
For in the arms of surrender,
We step into the light.

With every tear, a story,
Of love that once was whole,
In the act of simply letting,
We find the truth of soul.

Fortress of Faithful Hearts

In the realm where hope resides,
We build a fortress strong and true,
Made of faith and love united,
A refuge ever new.

Each heartbeat guards our essence,
Each prayer holds us tight,
In the fortress of faithful hearts,
We brave the darkest night.

Walls adorned with trust and kindness,
Windows shining purest grace,
In this sacred, shared devotion,
We find our rightful place.

Together, we stand unwavering,
Facing storms, we shall not fall,
For in the strength of unity,
We answer love's great call.

So let this fortress ever flourish,
A beacon through the years,
In the light of faithful hearts,
We gather hope, not fears.

Between the Leaves of Forgiveness

In the shade where mercy grows,
Hearts mend softly, like new pillows.
Whispers of grace in every breeze,
Healing wounds, putting hearts at ease.

Carried on wings of sacred prayer,
We learn to seek, to truly care.
Across the shadows, love outshines,
Between the leaves, His light defines.

Each step we take, hand in hand,
Together, we rise, together we stand.
Forgiveness blooms in sacred ground,
In unity, our strength is found.

As rivers flow to oceans wide,
Let go of burdens we need not hide.
In every rustle, His voice we hear,
A promise kept, forever near.

In every heart, a gentle plea,
To be set free, to truly see.
With every leaf that falls, we rise,
Forgiveness sought beneath the skies.

Unity in the Divine Tapestry

Threads of light weave through the night,
 Binding us in love's pure might.
 Each soul a pattern, bright and bold,
 In sacred stories, truth is told.

As we gather, faith interlaced,
 In harmony, our fears erased.
 Together we stand, hearts entwined,
 In the fabric of God, all aligned.

Every stitch, a prayer in space,
 Creating beauty, woven grace.
 Faith's colors burst, vibrant and true,
 Painting the world in heavenly hue.

With open hearts and hands held tight,
 We walk united towards the light.
 In every tear, joy's gentle trace,
 Love sustains us in this embrace.

Each moment shared, a sacred thread,
 In divine love, we find our bed.
 Together in faith, we rise and sing,
 Unity in Christ, our everything.

Serenade of the Selfless Soul

In the stillness, a heart unfolds,
A melody of love that never grows old.
In service bright, the spirit soars,
A selfless song in kindness pours.

Each act of love, a note divine,
In harmony with the grand design.
Hands reaching out, souls set free,
In the symphony of unity.

With gentle whispers, the world we mend,
A serenade for every friend.
Together we rise, together we give,
In the grace of love, we truly live.

Every smile shared, a spark ignites,
Lighting the path on darkest nights.
In the vibration of hearts that sing,
Selflessness blooms, a sacred spring.

Oh, let the chorus echo wide,
In every heart, let love abide.
Through selfless acts, may we be whole,
In the serenade of the selfless soul.

With Open Arms to the Divine

With open arms, we seek the light,
In the shadowed vale, we find our sight.
Each prayer a bridge, a sacred plea,
To embrace the love that sets us free.

In moments still, in quiet grace,
We find the warmth of His embrace.
He walks beside us, ever near,
In every heartbeat, love sincere.

As we rise with the morning sun,
Grateful for all that's yet to come.
In faith, we journey, hand in hand,
Trusting the path, the Master planned.

With every doubt, a stone unturned,
In the fires of hope, our spirits burned.
Reaching for Heaven, a soul's ascent,
With open arms, our hearts relent.

So let us gather, hearts ablaze,
In love's eternal, radiant haze.
With open arms, we greet the day,
To dance in the light, to find our way.

A Love Letter Written in the Stars

In the night, the heavens gleam,
Whispers soft, like a sacred dream.
Each twinkling light, a love letter,
Binding souls, now and forever.

Galaxies swirl, in divine embrace,
Echoes of love in this timeless space.
Threads of fate, woven so tight,
Guiding us home through endless night.

The moonlight dances on paths we tread,
Illuminating truths that love has said.
Stars align with each tender sigh,
A cosmic promise that will never die.

In silence, the universe bears witness,
To our love, pure and endless bliss.
Each heartbeat a beacon, shining bright,
A love letter written in celestial light.

Together we soar, through cosmic skies,
Infinite realms where our spirits rise.
Hand in hand, in divine accord,
In the stars, we find our Lord.

The Blessed Union of Two Souls

Two souls entwined, in sacred grace,
A blessed union in this holy space.
With faith as their guide, they walk as one,
Under the gaze of the shining sun.

Hearts open wide, like petals unfold,
Stories of love, in whispers told.
In every trial and every prayer,
Their bond grows stronger, love's tender care.

Guided by light, in darkness they stand,
A divine tether, forever hand in hand.
Through storms and shadows, they find the way,
In the warmth of love, night turns to day.

Together they rise, on wings of trust,
In the sacred dance of love, they must.
Each glance a promise, each touch a vow,
A blessed union, eternally now.

With every heartbeat, they nurture and grow,
In their garden of love, sweet blessings flow.
Rooted in faith, they flourish and bloom,
Two souls united, dispelling all gloom.

Cherishing the Divine Within Us

In every heart, a spark divine,
A sacred flame, forever shines.
To cherish the light is to find the truth,
In the depths of our souls, lies eternal youth.

Embrace the whispers of the holy grace,
In each moment, seek the sacred space.
Awaken the spirit, let love's song play,
In the dance of life, we find our way.

Each voice a hymn, each action a prayer,
Threads of connection, binding us where
Compassion flows, and kindness reigns,
In the garden of life, love breaks all chains.

Let every soul shine, in its unique hue,
A tapestry woven, me and you.
In unity's heart, we find our place,
Cherishing the divine in every face.

Together we rise, in harmony's call,
Embracing our gifts, we'll never fall.
For in our spirits, the truth does gleam,
Cherishing the divine, we live the dream.

Graced Pathways of Heartfelt Journeys

On graced pathways, we travel the night,
With hope in our hearts, we seek the light.
Each step a blessing, each breath a prayer,
In the journey of souls, we find what's rare.

Through valleys low and mountains high,
We hold each other and reach for the sky.
In laughter and tears, our spirits rise,
Bound by the love that never denies.

The road unwinds, with twists and turns,
For wisdom's flame, in our hearts still burns.
In every struggle, a lesson appears,
Guided by faith, we conquer our fears.

As we wander this sacred terrain,
In the echoes of love, we break every chain.
Together we walk, in joy and in sorrow,
Graced pathways leading to a bright tomorrow.

In the tapestry woven, our stories blend,
With love as the thread that will never end.
Each journey we take, a step closer to grace,
On graced pathways, we find our place.

A Journey into Sacred Wholeness

In the stillness of dawn's first light,
We wander paths of grace and sight,
Each step a prayer into the morn,
With hearts uplifted, souls reborn.

The whispers of the ancients call,
Echoes of love that never fall,
In unity, our souls entwined,
Embracing truths that we shall find.

The river flows with sacred dreams,
In its embrace, the spirit gleams,
Journey forth, let worries cease,
In every heartbeat, find your peace.

Mountains rise, steadfast and tall,
Their shadows stretch as we enthrall,
Upon their heights, the heavens meet,
In silence, find the grace so sweet.

With open hearts, we gather near,
In love's embrace, we cast off fear,
Together in this sacred dance,
We weave our lives, a blessed chance.

Under the Canopy of Trust

Beneath the boughs of hopeful trees,
We gather strength upon the breeze,
In nature's arms, we find our place,
A tapestry of love and grace.

The heavens stretch, a canvas bright,
Where stars ignite the cloak of night,
Each whispered prayer like gentle rain,
Filling our hearts, dissolving pain.

In unity, our spirits rise,
A chorus joining with the skies,
Within this sacred, tranquil space,
We nurture faith and seek embrace.

As seasons change, so do our ways,
In trust we walk through all our days,
With every step, the path unveils,
Unfurling love that never fails.

Together, in the light we stand,
Supporting one another's hand,
Under this canopy so wide,
We find our strength, our sacred guide.

An Offering Beyond Measure

In quiet moments of the heart,
We gather hopes, a sacred art,
With open hands, we share our fears,
An offering filled with silent tears.

Each breath we take, a gift divine,
The pulse of life, a holy line,
In this communion, love unfolds,
A treasure more than silver or gold.

We give our laughter, joy's bright song,
Intertwined with pains that feel so wrong,
Every moment shared, a precious thread,
In the tapestry where souls are fed.

With faith that moves the depths of night,
We find our way towards the light,
In every word, an echo lives,
Of boundless love that freely gives.

Let our hearts be open wide,
In this sacred space, we abide,
An offering, the truest measure,
Is love, the everlasting treasure.

Hearts Alight in Sacred Union

In the circle of this sacred flame,
We gather close, united, the same,
Each heart ignited, spirits soar,
In the light of love, we yearn for more.

With every glance, a knowing grace,
In silence shared, we find our place,
Together weaving dreams of old,
A story of love, beautifully bold.

In the embrace of kindred souls,
We dance to rhythms that make us whole,
With laughter rich and sorrows shared,
In trust, we find that we are cared.

The whispers of the universe sing,
In harmony, our spirits cling,
In every challenge, hand in hand,
Supporting one another to stand.

Hearts alight, a beacon bright,
Guiding us through the darkest night,
In this union, we are free,
Bound by love's sweet symmetry.

Love's Testament in Trials Faced

In shadows deep, our hearts unite,
Through storms we bear, in faith, we fight.
Each trial forms a stronger bond,
In love's embrace, we're deeply fond.

When sorrow knocks, let kindness flow,
In whispered prayers, our spirits grow.
Through heavy nights, we find the dawn,
In love's great test, we carry on.

With every tear, a lesson learned,
Through pain and joy, our souls are turned.
In every valley, hope's light beams,
We forge ahead, igniting dreams.

So let us stand, with hands held tight,
In love's pure glow, we find the light.
For when we face our dark despair,
Together, love, we always share.

A Vessel for Hopeful Affection

In tranquil waters, peace we seek,
With hearts aglow, our spirits speak.
A vessel forged in love's own fire,
Through trials faced, we rise higher.

The gentle winds of faith do guide,
When tempests rage, we turn inside.
In every wave, a prayer is cast,
For love's sweet grace, forever vast.

With open arms, we greet each day,
In hopeful hearts, we find our way.
A tender touch, a listening ear,
In every moment, love draws near.

So let us sail through life's great sea,
With love as anchor, strong and free.
No storm can shake our steadfast course,
Together bound, we feel love's force.

Sacred Reflections in the Depths of Trust

In silent prayer, we seek the truth,
In every heart beats tender youth.
A sacred bond, unbroken, pure,
In trust we find, our hearts endure.

Each whispered word, a promise made,
In brightened paths, our fears allayed.
Through joyful cries and deepest sighs,
In love's embrace, our spirits rise.

The mirror shows our soul's true face,
In sacred light, we find our place.
With every flaw, a chance to grow,
In trust's warm glow, we learn to know.

So let us weave our dreams anew,
In bonds of trust, our life rings true.
In every trial, our hearts align,
A sacred dance, forever divine.

The Eternal Flame of Devotion

In darkest nights, your light will shine,
With every breath, our hearts entwine.
An eternal flame, unwavering bright,
In love's warm glow, we find our sight.

With every step, our spirits soar,
Through life's vast sea, we crave for more.
A bond unbroken, sacred and true,
In devotion's call, I turn to you.

When silence falls, our hearts still speak,
In every glance, the love we seek.
Through trials faced and joy embraced,
In devotion's grip, we find our place.

Together we rise, through joy and strife,
In every moment, we share this life.
The flame of love, forever bright,
A beacon guiding us through the night.

Sanctified Touch of Longing Hearts

In quiet prayer, our souls unite,
With every hope, we seek the light.
A gentle whisper fills the air,
In sacred bonds, we find our care.

The stars above, they shine so bright,
Reminding us of love's pure sight.
Each heartbeat echoes, soft and true,
In longing hearts, our love renews.

Through trials faced, we stand as one,
With faith entwined, our race begun.
Your touch, a balm, upon my soul,
In sacred love, we are made whole.

As rivers flow, our spirits blend,
In holy grace, we find our end.
With every tear, a lesson learned,
In sanctified love, our hearts burned.

Through every storm, our spirits soar,
In love's embrace, we seek no more.
With every breath, we rise above,
In longing hearts, we find our love.

The Offering of a Fragile Heart

A fragile heart, we lay in trust,
In humble hands, we turn to dust.
With open arms, we share our fears,
In offering, we shed our tears.

In quiet moments, prayers arise,
With every hope, we reach the skies.
A sacred vow, in silence bound,
In fragile love, our strength is found.

Through winds of doubt, we hold on tight,
In shadows deep, we find the light.
This offering, our spirits bare,
In honesty, the truth we share.

With gentle touch, we mend the broken,
In tender words, our love is spoken.
A fragile heart, yet strong with grace,
In every trial, we find our place.

As dawn awakens, hope reborn,
In fragile hearts, we feel no scorn.
The offering, a light that shines,
In every bond, our love entwines.

Hearts Unbroken by Fear's Whisper

With courage found in faith so bright,
We walk unscathed through darkest night.
In whispers low, our fears may dance,
Yet hearts unbroken seek romance.

The path we tread is lined with grace,
With every step, we find our place.
In unity, we rise and stand,
With love's embrace, we join hands.

A fortress built on trust and hope,
In trials faced, we learn to cope.
Through storms that rage, we stand as one,
In hearts unbroken, fear is done.

Each heartbeat tells a story true,
In sacred love, we start anew.
With every dream, we cast aside,
In hearts unbroken, we abide.

Together strong, our spirits sing,
In every breath, a gift we bring.
With strength renewed, we face the day,
In hearts unbroken, love will stay.

A Covenant of Unsung Affection

In whispers soft, a promise made,
A quiet bond that will not fade.
With every glance, our hearts align,
In unsung affection, love will shine.

The vows we speak without a sound,
In simple gestures, hope is found.
With every heartbeat, truth unfolds,
A covenant of love, untold.

In gentle touches, words unspoken,
In silent prayers, our hearts unbroken.
Together we tread, through stormy seas,
In this sweet dance, our spirits ease.

A sacred trust we place in fate,
In every sigh, our souls await.
With open hearts, we seek the dawn,
In covenant made, our fears are gone.

With every step, we forge our way,
In unsung affection, brave we stay.
Together facing what may come,
In love's embrace, we find our home.

Blossoms of Grace in the Storm

In trials we stand, faith like the dawn,
Amidst the tempest, our fears are drawn.
Yet petals unfold, soft whispers of peace,
In storms we find strength, and turmoil will cease.

With each thunder's roar, hope's light shall break,
Through darkest of nights, a new path we make.
In the heart of the storm, our spirits ignite,
Blossoms of grace, a testament bright.

Hold fast to the promise, in shadows we'll bloom,
The fragrance of love, dispelling all gloom.
Together we rise, through sorrow, we learn,
In faith we are nourished, our spirits will burn.

A tapestry woven of tears and of mirth,
In challenges faced, we find our true worth.
With petals as banners, we dance in the rain,
For blossoms of grace, through trials, we gain.

Sacred Bonds of the Soul

In the quiet of night, our spirits entwine,
Sacred and pure, in a moment divine.
Hearts beating softly, in rhythmic embrace,
Together we journey, through time and through space.

Each whisper of love, a promise renewed,
In shadows we gather, in gratitude imbued.
Threads of connection, invisible grace,
In the fabric of life, we each find our place.

With hands clasped in prayer, we rise and we stand,
United as one, in this sacred land.
From ashes of doubt, we bloom in the light,
Miracles forged, in the depth of the night.

The song of our souls, a hymn from above,
In laughter and trials, the language of love.
Together we flourish, like stars in the sky,
In sacred bonds formed, we shall never die.

When Spirits Dance in Unity

Beneath the vast skies, where dreams intertwine,
In rhythm and pulse, our spirits align.
Each heartbeat a note in the melody's flow,
When spirits dance freely, true blessings will grow.

In circles of light, we gather as one,
With laughter and joy, our burdens undone.
Hands raised in gratitude, we sway to the song,
Together in unity, where we all belong.

In the stillness of dawn, when hope breaks anew,
We find our rejoicing, in all that we do.
In moments of silence, we hear the decree,
When spirits dance bravely, we set our hearts free.

The tapestry woven with threads of pure gold,
In love's soft embrace, a story retold.
As stars twinkle bright, in the canvas of night,
When spirits unite, all darkness takes flight.

Offering Our Hearts to the Divine

In whispers of prayer, our hearts we release,
To the heavens above, we seek gentle peace.
With open arms wide, we offer our souls,
In the light of the Divine, our shattered hearts whole.

With each breath we take, a promise we share,
In the love of the Spirit, we find solace there.
Through valleys of doubt, our faith gently soars,
In the presence of grace, our spirit restores.

Together we gather, as pilgrims of light,
Each moment a blessing, making dark into bright.
The whispers of hope, like angels would sing,
Offering our hearts, to the love that they bring.

In unity's strength, we traverse the unknown,
In the arms of the Divine, we never are alone.
With dreams intertwined, our purpose we find,
Offering our hearts, to the love that is kind.

A Garden Tended with Gentle Hearts

In the soil where kindness grows,
Each seed a prayer, softly sown.
With tender hands we weed the woes,
In this sacred place, love is known.

Sunlight dances on blooming grace,
The fragrance of hope fills the air.
Each flower a glimpse of Your face,
In the garden, we find You there.

Patience nurtures the hidden seed,
Each droplet of rain a blessing sent.
In vibrant colors, we see the need,
For hearts united, our love unbent.

With every harvest, joy unfolds,
Songs of gratitude weave through the rows.
In this garden, a story told,
Of gentle hearts where compassion grows.

So here we gather, hand in hand,
To celebrate the gifts we've shared.
With faith we flourish, we understand,
In this sacred space, love is bared.

Lovelight Shines in Sacred Spaces

In the silence, whispers of grace,
Lovelight trickles, pure and bright.
Hearts intertwine in this holy place,
Basking gently in shared light.

Beneath the arch of ancient trees,
We gather close, souls intertwining.
With open hearts, we feel the breeze,
A touch divine, love defining.

The glow of faith ignites our way,
Each moment cherished, a sacred gift.
In unity, we find our stay,
In every heartbeat, spirits lift.

With every prayer, we create a spark,
Lovelight radiates through the night.
In each shadow, we glimpse the arc,
Of divine love's eternal flight.

From our hearts, may the light flow,
In sacred spaces, may we embrace.
Together, in harmony, we grow,
In love's sweet warmth, we find our place.

The Divine Symphony of Connection

In each note, a story sung,
The symphony of hearts aligned.
In every chord, new life begun,
With faith as our guiding mind.

Melodies of love gently rise,
A chorus of voices, pure and clear.
In harmony, our spirits fly,
In this sacred space, You are near.

The rhythm of laughter fills the air,
Each heartbeat echoes with a call.
Together, we dance, free of care,
In the music, we rise and fall.

Each instrument plays a vital role,
The strings of compassion, soft and true.
Creating a tapestry for the soul,
A sacred blend, me and You.

As the symphony crescendos loud,
We surrender to the divine sea.
In this moment, we stand proud,
In Your love, we find unity.

Whispers of Faith in Tender Embrace

Soft whispers echo in the dawn,
A gentle breeze carries our hopes.
In tender embrace, fears are gone,
With faith, like a river, we cope.

Through trials and storms, we shall stand,
In unity, we gather near.
With open hearts and joined hands,
We journey forth, devoid of fear.

In quiet moments, souls align,
The warmth of kindness fuels our flame.
In faith's embrace, our spirits shine,
Our love, a constant, remains the same.

With every heartbeat, trust will bloom,
A garden nurtured by love's sweet song.
From shadows dark, we push through gloom,
With faith's light, we boldly belong.

As whispers soar, we lift our gaze,
The warmth of compassion guides our way.
In tender embrace, we sing Your praise,
With hearts entwined, forever we stay.

Unfurling the Petals of Affection

In the garden where love blooms,
Each petal whispers grace,
Tender hearts in sacred light,
United in a warm embrace.

Through the storms that come our way,
We stand firm, hand in hand,
A tapestry woven with dreams,
In His divine command.

With every prayer, our souls entwine,
Like vines that reach for the sky,
Together, we chase the dawn,
As time slips gently by.

Each gaze a spark of heaven's fire,
Illuminating our shared flight,
In love's simple, sacred dance,
We find strength in the night.

As petals unfold in the morn,
So too does our faith renew,
In the warmth of affection's glow,
We find life's essence true.

Sacred Bonds Defying the Night

In shadows deep where silence reigns,
Our hearts sing out in prayer,
With every whispered wish we send,
Faith lingers in the air.

Through trials lost and battles won,
A bond that time defies,
Together we shall face the dark,
With hope that never dies.

A lighthouse bright in stormy seas,
You guide me to the shore,
In sacred trust, we journey on,
Embracing evermore.

The stars above bear witness true,
To promises we keep,
In love's embrace, we find our way,
Awake when others sleep.

The night may fall, but we shall rise,
With courage, hand in hand,
In the heart of every struggle,
Together we shall stand.

Pilgrimage of Hearts Joined in Prayer

With humble steps, we journey forth,
In search of sacred grace,
Each heart a vessel of pure light,
Brought together in this space.

Through valleys low and mountains high,
Our souls unite as one,
In echoes of devotion's call,
Life's race is never done.

As we traverse this pilgrim path,
The Divine guides our way,
With every prayer, a deeper bond,
Our spirits rise and sway.

In moments filled with bliss and tears,
We carry one another,
In sacred trust, we boldly walk,
As sisters and as brothers.

The road ahead may twist and turn,
But love will light the night,
In our pilgrimage of hearts,
Together, we hold tight.

Echoes of Love in the Sacred Grove

In the grove where silence breathes,
A sacred hymn resounds,
Love's whispers weave through ancient trees,
Connecting all the grounds.

Beneath the sky, we gather close,
In unity, we stand,
Hearts entwined like roots below,
In this holy land.

Each echo speaks of dreams fulfilled,
Of laughter shared and tears,
In every moment, love reflects,
As time gently adheres.

With open arms, we rise in grace,
Embracing all that is,
In the sacred grove, we find our peace,
In love's eternal bliss.

So let us walk this path together,
With faith as our decree,
In echoes of love, forever bound,
In joy's sweet symphony.

The Language of Love in Prayer's Voice

In whispered tones we lift our hearts,
To heavens bright, where kindness imparts.
With every prayer, our souls unite,
A chorus sweet, in love's pure light.

Each word a thread, a sacred weave,
In faith we stand, and none shall grieve.
Together bound, in grace we find,
A language soft, transcending time.

Our sufferings shared, our joys embrace,
In humble praise, we seek His face.
For every tear, a lesson learned,
In love's great fire, our spirits burned.

As dawn unfolds, we rise anew,
In prayerful peace, our hearts imbue.
Through trials faced, in sorrow's grip,
We walk hand in hand, our faith a ship.

So let us sing, with voices clear,
In love's expanse, we cast out fear.
In prayer's embrace, our souls take flight,
The language of love, our guiding light.

Serene Waters of Trust and Affection

In stillness deep, the waters flow,
Reflecting love, as soft winds blow.
In tranquil depths, we find our peace,
With trust in hand, our worries cease.

Each ripple speaks, a gentle call,
In unity, we rise, not fall.
With every wave, a bond does form,
In love's embrace, we weather storm.

When shadows loom, and tempests roar,
Together we stand, on faith's shore.
In unity, our spirits soar,
As cherished hearts, we seek and store.

Let love abound, like rivers wide,
In every heart, let hope reside.
Through trials faced, and joy expressed,
In trust, we find our hearts at rest.

So let us drink from love's pure stream,
In every glance, a sacred dream.
With open arms, let affections reign,
In serene waters, forever gain.

Glorious Bonds in a World Divided

In a clash of tongues, our hearts align,
Through different paths, a love divine.
With open eyes, we see the light,
In glorious bonds, we share our plight.

No borders drawn can hold us back,
In every smile, we find a track.
As shadows fade, and doubts dispel,
In harmony, our spirits swell.

Each voice a note in heaven's song,
Together strong, we all belong.
With every step, a flame ignites,
In love's embrace, we reach new heights.

With hands entwined, we bridge the gap,
In every heart, a sacred map.
Through darkest nights, we find our way,
In glorious bonds, we choose to stay.

As time unfolds, our stories weave,
In love's embrace, we all believe.
In a world divided, together we rise,
With open hearts, we touch the skies.

In the Sanctuary of Togetherness

In quiet corners, where hearts convene,
A sacred space, like none have seen.
With arms wide open, we gather near,
In the sanctuary, love draws near.

With laughter shared, and sorrows told,
Each moment cherished, each heart bold.
In unity, we light the flame,
A bond unbroken, we stake our claim.

As seasons change, and years unfold,
In togetherness, our stories told.
With every glance, a promise made,
In love's embrace, our fears cascade.

Through trials faced, we stand as one,
In every storm, our love's not done.
With gentle strength, we lift each other,
In the sanctuary, we find our shelter.

So let us sing, in harmony's tune,
With open hands, we greet the moon.
In the sanctuary of every heart,
Together, we play our destined part.

Love's Pilgrimage Through Despair

In shadows deep where sorrow dwells,
The heart finds strength in silent wells.
With every tear, a prayer ascends,
A testament that love transcends.

Amidst the dark, a flicker shines,
A promise woven through divine signs.
With faith as compass, we journey on,
To find the light when hope seems gone.

In trials faced, our spirits grow,
Like seeds that burst from winter's snow.
Though paths are rugged, love remains,
A guiding star through all the pains.

Through valleys low and mountains high,
With every breath, we dare to fly.
For love, the flame that will not fade,
Turns every tear to comfort made.

In pilgrimage, our souls entwine,
Through every loss, we slowly shine.
For in despair, we find our way,
Towards love's embrace, come what may.

Treasures Buried in Kindness

In hearts of gold, compassion grows,
A gentle touch, a kindness shows.
The smallest act can spark the light,
To lift the soul and make it bright.

In every eye, a story lies,
Of struggles faced beneath the skies.
A smile shared, a hand to lend,
Reveals a love that has no end.

The treasure maps are drawn in grace,
With guiding stars at every place.
Through storms of life and winds of change,
Kindness blooms and feels no strange.

Each moment holds a chance to give,
To sow the seeds where hearts can live.
In every deed, our souls delight,
With kindness wrapped in purest light.

For buried deep, the treasure's found,
In loving hearts that spread around.
In kindness shared, our spirits soar,
A legacy of love and more.

Sunlight on the Waiting Heart

In silence deep, the heart does yearn,
For sunlight's grace, for love's return.
Through seasons passed, and dreams that dwell,
The waiting heart, a sacred well.

Each dawn unveils a glimmer bright,
A promise woven into light.
With every ray that warms the soul,
The waiting heart begins to whole.

In patient trust, the world unfolds,
As hope ignites, the future holds.
For in the wait, the spirit grows,
And love's sweet bloom forever shows.

Though shadows creep and doubts arise,
The steadfast heart will touch the skies.
For every tear, a seed is sown,
In time, the light will be our own.

So let the waiting be our song,
In trust we stand, where we belong.
With sunlight's kiss, the heart will sing,
In love's embrace, we find our spring.

Echoes of Grace in the Wilderness

In barren lands where whispers cease,
The echo of grace brings sweet release.
Through rugged paths and starlit nights,
It calls us forth to share our lights.

With every step, the heart will know,
That in the struggle blooms the growth.
For in the wild, the spirit thrives,
As grace unfolds, our hope arrives.

When fears arise and shadows loom,
The echoes guide, dispelling gloom.
For every trial, a chance to see,
The grace that sets our spirits free.

Within the wilderness, we roam,
But in our hearts, we find our home.
The echoes ring through every tear,
A promise made that love is near.

So let us wander, let us roam,
With echoes of grace, we shall not moan.
For in the wild, we find our way,
And in each heart, love's light will stay.

Divine Embrace Beyond Fear

In whispers soft, the spirit calls,
A light that breaks through darkest walls.
Fear not the night, for dawn shall rise,
In every tear, a prayer complies.

Heaven's hand, a gentle guide,
Through raging storms, we shall abide.
With faith, we tread the sacred path,
Embracing love, escaping wrath.

Trust in the heart, where hope ignites,
Each soul a star that brightly lights.
In unity, we find our grace,
Divine embrace, our sacred space.

Let go of doubt, let go of pain,
In every loss, His love remains.
Together we rise, forever near,
In every heartbeat, He draws near.

Eternal truth within us blooms,
Guided by light, dispelling glooms.
Fear falls away, as love ascends,
In His embrace, our spirit mends.

Faithful Beats in Shadows Bright

When shadows fall, we hear the song,
Of faithful hearts, united strong.
In darkest hours, our spirits cheer,
A melody of love draws near.

Together we dance, under the stars,
Healing the wounds, embracing scars.
In every pulse, a sacred beat,
Faith lights the path, our lives complete.

With courage deep, we face the night,
Transforming fear into pure light.
The grace of God, in whispers, flows,
In faithful hearts, true love grows.

Hope blooms anew, like morning dew,
In every loss, we find what's true.
Together we stand, hand in hand,
In light and love, our lives are planned.

Faithful we rise, through trials we soar,
In shadows bright, we seek to explore.
With open hearts, our spirits tight,
We find our strength in love's pure light.

Embracing Grace Amidst Trials

In trials faced, we find our might,
Each struggle leads us to the light.
With open arms, we dance with fate,
In grace we stand, through every gate.

The journey bends, but never breaks,
In whispered prayers, our spirit wakes.
Every challenge, a chance to grow,
In love's embrace, we learn to glow.

As storms may rage, our hearts remain,
In faith and trust, we bear the strain.
For in the dark, a spark ignites,
A guiding star, that shines so bright.

Together we rise, with courage true,
In every breath, a glimpse of you.
Each moment precious, a gift divine,
In trials embraced, our souls align.

Embracing grace, we walk the line,
A tapestry of love, entwined.
With every step, we leave behind,
The weight of fear; in joy we find.

Soulmates in the Light of Devotion

In sacred bonds, our souls align,
Together we shine, in love divine.
With every gaze, a silent vow,
In light of devotion, we humbly bow.

Through whispered dreams, our spirits soar,
In unity, our hearts explore.
The path ahead, with joy adorned,
In love's embrace, we are reborn.

With gentle hands, we heal each scar,
Soulmates we are, no distance far.
In every challenge, we stand as one,
Illuminated by the morning sun.

Our laughter dances, a sacred tune,
In blissful nights, beneath the moon.
In every moment, we find our grace,
Soulmates forever, in love's embrace.

Through trials faced and victories gained,
In life's great tapestry, our love remains.
Devotion's fire, a beacon bright,
Together we walk, into the light.

Trust's Embrace: A Spiritual Voyage

In the stillness, faith does rise,
Guiding hearts beneath vast skies.
Every step, a sacred call,
Trusting Him, we stand tall.

Waves of doubt may crash and break,
Yet in His arms, our fears forsake.
Through the storms, His light shall gleam,
In trust's embrace, we find our dream.

Mountains high and valleys deep,
In His promise, our souls do leap.
With each breath, we seek the way,
A voyage bright, come what may.

Hands uplifted, spirits soar,
In unity, we ask for more.
As pilgrims on this path we tread,
In trust's embrace, we're gently led.

Let our hearts with love ignite,
Guided forward towards the light.
In every trial, His hand we trace,
Finding peace in trust's embrace.

A Symphony of Hearts in Divine Rhythm

In the silence, melodies bloom,
Whispers of love dispel the gloom.
Voices rise in harmony's song,
In this symphony, we belong.

Each heartbeat a note, pure and clear,
Echoing grace, casting out fear.
Together we weave a tapestry,
Of faith and hope in unity.

In the chapel of the open skies,
Our spirits dance as the soul flies.
With every prayer, we intertwine,
Creating a rhythm, divine design.

Hands lifted high in gratitude's grace,
Melodies warming every place.
In the heart's chamber, light ignites,
This symphony guides through darkest nights.

As dawn reveals a brand new day,
We celebrate love's endless sway.
In this sacred bond we find rest,
A symphony of hearts, truly blessed.

In the Temple of Hope and Yearning

Within these walls, our spirits rise,
Amidst the whispers, dreams surmise.
In the temple made of light,
We gather strength to face the night.

Prayers like incense fill the air,
Yearning hearts laid bare with care.
Each tear we shed, a sacred stream,
Woven with faith, we dare to dream.

In moments still, His presence near,
Binds our troubles, calms our fear.
In this haven of hope and grace,
We find our solace, our rightful place.

With open hearts, we seek Him still,
Trusting in love, aligning will.
In the sacred silence, peace we glean,
In the temple's embrace, hope is seen.

As we depart, a flame ignites,
Carrying warmth through darkest nights.
In every step, His love we yearn,
In this sacred space, we always return.

Celestial Bonds of Kindred Spirits

In the dance of starlit skies,
Kindred spirits rise and fly.
Bound together, heart to heart,
In this journey, we shall never part.

Emanating love from deep within,
We embrace each loss and win.
In sacred circles, laughter glows,
Sharing wisdom, as our spirit grows.

Every soul, a shining guide,
Illuminating where love resides.
With every story, faith restores,
Celestial bonds open new doors.

Through trials faced and burdens shared,
In unity, our spirits bared.
Hand in hand, we walk the way,
In kindred hearts, we find our stay.

As dawn unfolds its golden rays,
These bonds of love shall never fade.
In the tapestry of the divine,
Celestial connections, forever shine.

Trusting the Unseen

In shadows deep, I walk with faith,
A whisper calls, it lights my path.
The stars above, they guide my way,
In silence speaks the dawn of day.

Each breath a prayer, each heartbeat grace,
In every trial, I find His face.
The unseen hands, they hold me tight,
My doubts dissolve in love's pure light.

With open eyes, I seek the truth,
In every moment, eternal youth.
The promise waits in every sigh,
For in His arms, I learn to fly.

Though storms may rage and shadows loom,
I stand secure, dispelling gloom.
For in the dark, His peace remains,
In trust I thrive, beyond the chains.

Faith is my anchor, hope my sail,
Through unknown waters, love won't fail.
I trust the unseen, forever near,
In every heartbeat, He is here.

Prayer of the Open Heart

In quiet corners, hearts awake,
With every breath, a vow we make.
A song of love, a gentle plea,
In every moment, set us free.

Oh, listen close, oh, hear our cry,
With arms extended, we reach high.
The sacred bond, it knows no end,
In each shared tear, a heart to mend.

With every word, we seek the light,
A touch divine to guide our sight.
Our spirits rise, His will in tow,
Through open hearts, His blessings flow.

In gratitude, we lay us bare,
Entrust our dreams to gentle care.
As faith ignites, our souls take flight,
In love's embrace, we find the light.

Awakened hearts, united strong,
In every trial, we sing our song.
The path is clear, our spirits soar,
In prayer of love, we seek no more.

Love's Radiance Through Trials

When shadows fall and doubts arise,
In love's embrace, our spirit flies.
Though storms may come, we stand as one,
In unity, our victory's won.

Each challenge faced, a sacred gift,
Through trials hard, our souls will lift.
In darkest hours, our light will gleam,
For love prevails, a steadfast dream.

The fire of hope, it warms the night,
In every struggle, find the light.
With hearts aligned, we rise above,
In trials faced, we prove our love.

Through every tear, strength intertwines,
In love's embrace, our spirit shines.
We walk by faith, not by the sight,
In love's radiance, we find our light.

Together bound, our voices strong,
In love's great hymn, we all belong.
With each new dawn, our hearts will sing,
Through trials faced, love's true offering.

Beneath the Veil of Fear

Across the chasm, shadows creep,
Beneath the veil, our fears run deep.
But in the silence, courage grows,
Through darkest nights, a bright light flows.

The heart that trembles seeks to heal,
In sacred whispers, we reveal.
A strength within, a guiding spark,
To pierce the veil, dispel the dark.

With every step, we face the fright,
In love's embrace, we find the might.
From sorrow's grasp, we shall be free,
Through every challenge, we shall see.

Emerge from fear, embrace the grace,
For every tear, He'll interlace.
In trust we stand, no more to hide,
Beneath the veil, love is our guide.

With open hearts, we rise anew,
In faith and hope, all things we do.
Together strong, we will endure,
Beneath the veil, love is the cure.

The Light Within the Shadows

In darkness deep, a whisper calls,
A flicker shines where silence falls.
Through trials faced, we seek the grace,
The light within, a sacred place.

Amidst the night, His presence near,
A balm for wounds, our hearts revere.
With every tear that falls like rain,
We find His joy amidst the pain.

From shadows cast, He lifts our sight,
To guide us through the endless night.
In every breath, a chance to see,
The hope that lives eternally.

As dawn breaks forth, the shadows flee,
His love revealed, our spirits free.
In every heart, a flame ignites,
The light within, our true delights.

Embrace the glow, let fear depart,
For in His warmth, we find our heart.
The shadows fade, His truth resounds,
In every soul, His love abounds.

Anointed by Vulnerability's Gift

In brokenness, a strength is born,
Through wounds that bare our hearts, we mourn.
Yet in this place, His love does seep,
Anointed grace, our souls to keep.

With open hands, we share our scars,
Reflecting light like distant stars.
This vulnerability, a path divine,
To heal the soul, through love we shine.

Each tear a river, flowing wide,
A testament of faith, our guide.
With every bruise, a lesson learned,
In the depths of pain, His light returned.

When courage wanes and shadows creep,
In His embrace, our burdens steep.
For in the cracks, the beauty flows,
The strength of love perpetually grows.

Through trembling hearts, His whispers flow,
A call to rise, and gently grow.
Anointed by the gifts we bare,
In Jesus' name, we're healed from despair.

Wings of Redemption

Upon the winds, our spirits soar,
With faith as wings, we long for more.
Through trials faced, we learn to trust,
In every heart, His love is just.

From ashes rise, our prayers ignite,
In brokenness, we seek the light.
With every step, the path unfolds,
A story penned in grace so bold.

With wings of hope, we take to flight,
From darkest nights to dawn's pure light.
In every challenge, we feel His hand,
Guiding our hearts to the promised land.

So lift your gaze, let fear depart,
For in His love, we find our heart.
Through valleys deep, our spirits climb,
In wings of redemption, we rise sublime.

Together we stand, a force renewed,
In unity, our faith imbued.
With hearts ablaze and spirits free,
In Christ's embrace, we're meant to be.

Elysium Found in Tenderness

In gentle whispers, love unfolds,
A sacred warmth, a truth retold.
In tender hearts, His grace is sown,
A paradise where love has grown.

Through every touch, a promise made,
In acts of kindness, fear will fade.
So let us walk with open eyes,
To see the grace in each sunrise.

Elysium found in every smile,
A healing balm, our hearts beguile.
In laughter shared and tears embraced,
His loving presence, our fears erased.

With hands outstretched, we gather near,
To lift each other, to persevere.
In every moment, a chance to share,
The tenderness that lingers there.

For love prevails through storms and tears,
In sacred bonds, we cast our fears.
Elysium found in pure embrace,
In tender hearts, we seek His grace.

Everlasting Light in the Depths

In shadows deep where whispers flow,
The light of grace begins to glow.
With every step through trials faced,
The heart of love cannot be erased.

Through darkest nights our spirits rise,
Embraced by hope, the soul complies.
A beacon bright, a guiding star,
Forever near, no matter how far.

In depths of sorrow, peace will find,
The everlasting light confined.
In faith we walk, in truth we stand,
Together held by loving hands.

As dawn breaks forth, the shadows flee,
In unity, we find the key.
With open hearts, we shine so bright,
In every soul, the everlasting light.

Eternally bound by sacred trust,
In Divine love, we live, we must.
Through trials faced and burdens borne,
In light we rise, again reborn.

Sacred Visions of Shared Dreams

In silent prayers, our souls align,
With visions bright, a light divine.
Together we weave our hopes anew,
In sacred dreams, we find our view.

With lifted hearts, we journey forth,
In reverence deep, embracing worth.
A tapestry of faith we share,
Entwined in love, our spirits bare.

In every moment, grace unfolds,
As sacred visions gently hold.
The dreams we harbor blend as one,
A radiant path beneath the sun.

For in our hearts, each whisper sings,
The essence pure that faith still brings.
With every heartbeat, a promise made,
In shared dreams, our fears cascade.

Together we rise, unbroken, free,
In sacred visions, we find our key.
For love's embrace, forever holds,
The dreams that intertwine our souls.

The Bridge of Souls: Faithful Connection

Across the waters, a bridge we seek,
In whispers soft, the spirits speak.
With every heartbeat, faith prevails,
In gentle winds, our love exhales.

The threads of light that bind us close,
In every joy, in every woe.
With open arms, we face the storm,
In faithful connection, our lives transform.

Through trials faced, our hearts unite,
In sacred moments, day turns night.
Each soul a lantern, shining bright,
Together we navigate the night.

For in the silence, love speaks loud,
A faithful bond, forever proud.
With every scar, a story told,
The bridge of souls, a sight to behold.

As we walk on, hand in hand,
In love's embrace, we make our stand.
Faithful connection, never stray,
In every heartbeat, night and day.

Beneath the Veil of Divine Protection

Under the stars, where shadows dwell,
In quiet whispers, our hearts compel.
Beneath the veil, where love ignites,
Divine protection graces our nights.

Through storms we sail, with courage bright,
In every trial, we seek the light.
With every prayer, a shield we raise,
In sacred trust, our spirits blaze.

In gentle whispers, angels tread,
Guiding our path, where souls are led.
With open hearts, we find our way,
In every dawn, a brand new day.

With grateful hearts, we face the dawn,
In divine protection, never withdrawn.
For every tear that's softly shed,
Is met with love, the spirit fed.

In harmony, our voices blend,
Beneath the veil, love shall defend.
In unity, we rise and stand,
In faith we find, a guiding hand.

Hallelujahs in the Valley of Trust

In the valley low, hearts do rise,
With hymns of hope that touch the skies.
Each moment whispers, God is near,
In shadows deep, His light is clear.

Together we'll walk this sacred ground,
With every step, His love is found.
Through trials faced, our faith will sing,
Hallelujahs soar on angel wing.

When storms may rage, and fears may creep,
In His embrace, our souls will leap.
Trust in Him, for He will guide,
In His warm grace, we will abide.

A path adorned with blessings sweet,
In every heartbeat, His love we meet.
Let praises rise, like incense strong,
In the valley of trust, we all belong.

With each new dawn, our spirits bloom,
In light of faith, we conquer gloom.
Hallelujahs chime, our hearts unite,
In the valley of trust, we find our light.

The Shield of Faithful Kindness

In a world where silence often reigns,
Let kindness flow like gentle rains.
A shield of faith in every heart,
Compassion's touch, a sacred art.

When burdens weigh, lift them with love,
A soft embrace, a sign from above.
Through trials shared, our spirits rise,
In tender moments, God's grace lies.

With every act, let kindness spread,
As faithful hearts, our hope is fed.
In quiet strength, our voices blend,
Together we heal, together we mend.

Let not the darkness steal our grace,
For in our hearts, we'll find a place.
The shield of kindness, forever strong,
In the dance of faith, we all belong.

So let us walk with heads held high,
Under His wings, we'll never die.
With kindness firm, our spirits soar,
In a world of love, forevermore.

A Rosary of Eternal Sentiments

Each bead a prayer, a whispered sigh,
In love's embrace, our spirits fly.
Through every joy, and every tear,
The rosary binds us ever near.

Like golden threads in sacred light,
Eternal sentiments shining bright.
In every heart, a story shared,
In every moment, God has cared.

With faith entwined, we seek the truth,
In childhood dreams and fervent youth.
The sacred pact of love we weave,
A gentle touch in which we believe.

So let our prayers ascend like smoke,
In the still of night, the heart awoke.
Together we stand, hand in hand,
A rosary of faith, forever grand.

The light of love, a guiding star,
From heaven above, we're never far.
In eternal bonds, our spirits dwell,
In the sacred silence, all is well.

Love's Sanctuary in a World Unkind

In a world where shadows seem to grow,
Love's sanctuary lights the way we go.
With open hearts, let kindness shine,
In tender moments, we intertwine.

When hope seems lost, let love arise,
A beacon bright in twilight skies.
Each gentle word, a soothing balm,
In love's embrace, our hearts are calm.

Though storms may rage and doubts may creep,
In faith we stand, His promise keep.
A sanctuary built on trust and care,
In love's embrace, we are aware.

Let's speak our truth with voices clear,
In every moment, draw Him near.
Together we rise, our hearts entwined,
In love's sanctuary, the lost will find.

In acts of grace, our spirits soar,
In unity, we seek to restore.
So let love flourish, let joy unfold,
In this sanctuary, hearts grow bold.

Wings of Devotion Lift Us High

In twilight's grace, our spirits soar,
With whispers soft, we seek the shore.
Each prayer a feather, each hope a plea,
Together we rise, forever to be.

Through trials thick, our faith will guide,
In sacred light, we shall abide.
Hand in hand, we trace the sky,
With wings of love, we lift up high.

In gratitude, we bow our heads,
As love's pure light the darkness shreds.
Together we stand, our hearts entwined,
In this holy bond, true peace we find.

For in the quiet, our souls ignite,
Each whispered prayer a beacon bright.
With every tear, we cleanse the soul,
In worship's arms, we find our whole.

So let us soar on wings divine,
In heaven's hymn, our hearts align.
With devotion's strength, we face the day,
Together in light, we find our way.

Divine Threads in the Tapestry of Two

In the loom of life, we weave our fate,
Each moment shared, a binding state.
With every stitch, our hearts combine,
In love's embrace, your hand in mine.

The sacred dance, our spirits twirl,
Two souls united, the tapestry unfurl.
Each joy and sorrow, a pattern rare,
Together we flourish, a bond to share.

The threads of grace, in colors bright,
Weaving joy, dispelling night.
In trials faced, our fibers taut,
In faith we trust, love's lessons taught.

Within this craft, we find our song,
In harmony sweet, we both belong.
With every breath, and every sigh,
Divine the bond that cannot die.

So let us cherish this woven dream,
In the fabric of love, we find our gleam.
Together we stand, forever true,
In life's great design, me and you.

Love's Anthem in Sacred Silence

In stillness deep, where whispers reign,
Love's gentle song breaks every chain.
In quiet realms, our spirits rise,
As sacred silence speaks the skies.

With every breath, a hymn is born,
In the hush of night, a new dawn's sworn.
In devotion's grace, our hearts align,
Bound in a rhythm, so pure, divine.

Each soft embrace, a sacred pledge,
In love's own light, we take the edge.
In moments shared, our souls take flight,
In love's warm embrace, we find the light.

The sacred silence wraps us whole,
In every beat, it fills the soul.
With whispered vows and silent prayers,
In sacred love, our spirit dares.

So let us dwell where quiet hums,
In love's sweet anthem, the heart succumbs.
In each tender gaze, a promise stays,
In sacred silence, our love displays.

Luminaries of a Faithful Heart

In the glow of faith, our hearts ignite,
As stars of hope emerge from night.
With every prayer, we lose the dark,
In love's embrace, we find the spark.

Together we shine, a radiant beam,
In the vast expanse, a shared dream.
With hands uplifted, we touch the sky,
In faithful hearts, we learn to fly.

Guided by light, we walk the path,
In the face of trials, we feel love's wrath.
With courage strong, we forge ahead,
In every word, His truth is spread.

As luminaries bright, we light the way,
In service shown, we humbly sway.
With every act of kindness shared,
In unity's strength, we know He cared.

So let us shine with love's pure grace,
In every challenge, find His face.
In the faithful heart, a light will spark,
Together we glow, forever in the dark.

A Tapestry Woven with Trust

In the loom of faith, we stand,
Each thread a prayer, each hand in hand.
Through trials bright and shadows deep,
We weave our hopes, in love we keep.

With hearts aligned, we journey forth,
Embracing light, affirming worth.
In whispered vows, our spirits soar,
A tapestry rich, forevermore.

Together we rise, in grace's arms,
Shielded safe from worldly harms.
Each knot a bond, our souls entwined,
In sacred trust, our paths aligned.

As we gather at the evening's close,
United in peace, like a blooming rose.
In quiet prayers, our hopes ignite,
A tapestry woven, pure and bright.

Let the threads of love endure,
In every heart, find faith secure.
Emboldened by the ties we share,
In trust we flourish, in trust we dare.

Blessings in Vulnerability's Veil

Underneath the stars we meet,
With open hearts, we find our seat.
In vulnerability, whispers glide,
A treasure found, no need to hide.

Each tear a blessing, each laugh divine,
In shared moments, our souls align.
Through every crack, light filters in,
In sacred spaces, we begin.

With courage found in tender grace,
We unfold truths, embrace our place.
In the strength of our softened skin,
We discover love, the depth within.

In the hush of night, we share our fears,
Wrapped in the warmth of our tears.
For in the rawness of our plight,
A blessing blooms, pure and bright.

Let not the weight of hurt confine,
For vulnerability's veil does shine.
In every heart, may love unveil,
The blessings held in vulnerability's trail.

Seraphim Whisper of Belonging

In the glow of dawn, soft voices sing,
Seraphim whisper of belonging.
With wings of light, they lift our cares,
In sacred circles, through layered prayers.

Every heartbeat, a sonorous hymn,
Together we rise, our spirits brim.
In laughter and tears, a bond we weave,
In unity's light, we truly believe.

Throughout the night, their songs bestow,
A gentle comfort, a steady glow.
In heavens above, we find our way,
Embraced in hope, come what may.

As we gather in love's pure embrace,
Seraphim guide us through time and space.
In joy and sorrow, we know we're home,
In their whispers, we no longer roam.

With each breath, we feel the grace,
In every heart, a sacred place.
Together we dance, in harmony's song,
For in belonging, we are forever strong.

Souls Merging Under Heaven's Gaze

Underneath the watchful skies,
Two souls interlace, love's reprise.
In gentle glances, truths unfold,
A story whispered, timeless and bold.

With every step, our spirits blend,
In this journey, we find a friend.
Through trials faced, we understand,
In togetherness, hearts expand.

Beneath the heavens, we spread our dreams,
In moonlight's glow, the world redeems.
The stars respond, a cosmic dance,
Two souls entwined in sacred chance.

In the hush of night, we share a vow,
Under heaven's gaze, we cherish now.
In unity, we breathe as one,
An endless story, just begun.

With love's embrace, we walk the path,
In laughter's melody, we seek the math.
Forever joined, come what may,
Souls merging under heaven's sway.

Divine Symphony of Hearts

In harmony we gather, souls entwined,
Voices raised, a chorus so divine.
Each note a prayer, from heart to heart,
In this symphony, we play our part.

The rhythm of grace, a gentle sway,
Echoes of love, guiding our way.
With each beat, we find our song,
In unity, we all belong.

Beneath the veil of night, stars align,
Mirrored lights, as souls intertwine.
In the quiet, whispers of hope,
Together we learn, together we cope.

In trials faced, we lift each other,
A bond so strong, like sister and brother.
Through shadows cast, we rise and shine,
A testament to love divine.

With every tear, a blessing flows,
In the garden of faith, compassion grows.
Tender hands that heal the pain,
In this sacred space, all is gained.

As we journey forth, hearts in tune,
Trusting the path, we follow the moon.
In the depths, where sorrow may dwell,
We find a light, in love we excel.

Beneath the Stars, We Unite

Under stars that shimmer, hearts align,
In the quiet night, our spirits shine.
A tapestry woven with threads of grace,
In the embrace of love, we find our place.

Voices soft as whispers, carry in the air,
Each confession shared, a sacred prayer.
Boundless hopes like constellations bright,
Guiding our souls through the darkest night.

In unison we stand, through trials we face,
Hands held together, we find our space.
With hearts that soar, we break every chain,
United in love, we will rise again.

Through the storms and struggles, we grow strong,
With faith as our anchor, we sing our song.
In this grand tapestry, each thread we weave,
A reminder of promise, a reason to believe.

Together we shine, like lanterns in the dark,
Illuminating paths, igniting the spark.
In the stillness of night, we find our way,
Beneath the stars, in love we stay.

Strength Found in Tenderness

In whispers soft, strength can be found,
In gentle embraces, love knows no bound.
Through trials faced, our spirits entwine,
In the arms of grace, our hearts align.

With every heartbeat, courage in sight,
In the shadows of pain, we seek the light.
Tenderness speaks, louder than words,
In the silence, our spirit is stirred.

Through tears and laughter, we share our woes,
In the garden of faith, compassion grows.
Each act of kindness, a seed to sow,
In the bloom of love, our souls will flow.

Together we rise, hands interlaced,
In moments of doubt, love is embraced.
In the journey of life, we stand side by side,
With tenderness guiding, our hearts open wide.

In the arms of each other, we find our place,
A refuge of warmth, a sacred space.
Through struggles endured, we emerge anew,
In strength found in tenderness, we see it true.

Embracing the Wounded Spirit

In shadows that linger, we find our way,
To cradle the broken, come what may.
With open arms, we gather near,
Embracing the wounded, drying each tear.

In spaces of hurt, we plant our feet,
Listening closely, hearts skip a beat.
With gentle hands, we mend and restore,
In the warmth of compassion, we find much more.

Holding the weary, we share their load,
Illuminating paths, lightening the road.
In each tender moment, we forge anew,
With love's gentle touch, we break through.

Together we rise, from ashes of pain,
In the tapestry of healing, hope will remain.
Through the trials we face, there's courage to leverage,
In embracing the spirit, we find our treasure.

With open hearts, we create a space,
For the weary travelers, a warm embrace.
In unity found, our spirits will soar,
Embracing the wounded, forevermore.

The Altar of Understanding

In quiet reverence we kneel,
The whispers of wisdom feel.
Hearts open wide to the truth,
Love's gentle touch renews our youth.

Each question posed, a sacred gate,
Guided by faith, we contemplate.
With humble hearts, we seek the light,
Illumined paths in the darkest night.

In the stillness, spirits soar,
Boundless grace forevermore.
Unity sings in harmonious grace,
Together, we find our true place.

Understanding blooms like a flower,
In the garden of God's power.
Through trials faced, we come to know,
The seeds of love we bravely sow.

So let us gather, hand in hand,
A tapestry woven, a sacred strand.
To the altar of wisdom, we're drawn,
In the light of hope, we rise with dawn.

With Grace We Rise

In dawn's embrace, we lift our eyes,
The sun igniting hopeful skies.
With grace, we rise on wings of prayer,
Trusting the love that's always there.

The trials faced, a sacred test,
In faith's arms, we find our rest.
Through valleys low, we tread with care,
The promise of light beyond despair.

With every step, we find our way,
In gratitude, we choose to stay.
Each moment blessed, a gift to hold,
In the warmth of love, our spirits bold.

Together we stand, unbreakably strong,
In the symphony of life's sweet song.
With open hearts, we share the light,
Guided by truth, dispelling night.

So let us rise, with faith as our song,
In the journey of love, where we belong.
With grace we gather, hand in hand,
In unity forged, we brightly stand.

Illuminated by Compassion's Flame

In every heart, a spark resides,
With compassion, the spirit guides.
Illuminated, souls intertwine,
In the warmth of love, we refine.

With gentle hands, we heal the pain,
In kindness shared, our strength we gain.
Through tears we water the seeds of hope,
Together we rise, learn, and cope.

The light of mercy, pure and bright,
Chases away the deepest night.
For every soul, a story told,
In love's embrace, we break the mold.

With open eyes, we see the need,
In acts of love, our hearts are freed.
Compassion's flame, a guide so true,
With open hearts, we start anew.

Let us gather 'round this sacred fire,
With every act, we reach higher.
In unity's bond, we rise each day,
Illuminated by love's pure way.

Surrendering to the Divine Design

In silence deep, we hear the call,
Surrendering all, we stand tall.
Trusting the path set before our feet,
In faith's embrace, our souls meet.

With open hearts, we yield control,
Letting the Spirit mend the whole.
In the ebb and flow of life's grand scheme,
We find our place, a sacred dream.

Each twist and turn, a lesson learned,
Through shadows cast, our hearts have yearned.
In surrendering, we find our peace,
In divine design, our worries cease.

With every breath, a divine decree,
In harmony with all, we're truly free.
In acceptance lies our greatest strength,
In trusting love, we find our length.

So let us walk with faith renewed,
In divine grace, we are imbued.
With open spirits, we shall rise,
Surrendering to love's pure ties.

In the Everlasting Light of Togetherness

In the embrace of dawn's gentle sight,
We gather hearts in the everlasting light.
Together we rise, hand in hand we stand,
A sacred bond woven by love's own strand.

In whispers of faith, our spirits unite,
With hopes like stars, shining through the night.
Each prayer a thread in our tapestry spun,
Together we journey, two souls become one.

Through valleys of doubt and mountains of grace,
With kindness and mercy, we find our place.
In laughter and tears, we share every part,
In the everlasting light, you dwell in my heart.

As seasons will change, still our promise remains,
A sanctuary built through joy and through pains.
In the echo of love, our voices repeat,
In the light of togetherness, our burdens grow sweet.

So let us rejoice in this divine embrace,
For in every moment, we discover our space.
Together we flourish, forever we bloom,
In the everlasting light, dispelling all gloom.

The Chapel of Shared Breath

In the chapel of shared breath, love takes its flight,
Where whispers of harmony shine ever bright.
Two souls intertwine in a sacred space,
Offering grace, boundless, we find our place.

With every heartbeat, a message is clear,
The language of trust, for in you, I'm near.
In silence, we marvel at stars up above,
In the chapel of shared breath, we nurture love.

Through storms and through trials, our spirits will soar,
For we walk this journey, leaving nevermore.
With faith as our guide, we shall not stray,
In this sacred embrace, together we stay.

In laughter and sorrow, a bond that won't break,
Our vows renewed with each step that we take.
With joy in our hearts, each moment we'll treasure,
In the chapel of shared breath, our souls find pleasure.

Let your spirit dance in this radiant glow,
As we cultivate love, in all that we sow.
In harmony's echo, this truth shall resound,
In the chapel of shared breath, love's peace shall be found.

A Pilgrim's Journey to Love's Altar

On a path made of dreams where the wildflowers grow,
A pilgrim ventures forth, with heart all aglow.
Each step tells a story, each moment a prayer,
To love's sacred altar, I journey with care.

Through valleys of doubt and mountains of grace,
With hope in my heart, I seek a safe space.
With each passing season, my spirit takes flight,
A pilgrim's journey to love's guiding light.

With lanterns of faith and a compass of trust,
I wander the world, as a dreamer I must.
Through shadows I search, for the warmth of your hand,
In love's sacred altar, together we stand.

As rivers will flow and the tides gently sway,
I carry your essence in each day's ballet.
With laughter and tears, we carve out our fate,
On this pilgrim's journey, love conquers all hate.

So let us rejoice in this sacred affair,
For love is the answer with riches to share.
With hearts intertwined, we ascend to the skies,
A pilgrim's journey to love's sweetest prize.

The Light of Trust Against All Doubt

In the darkness we wander, yet hope lights the way,
The light of trust shines bright, guiding each day.
With faith like a beacon, we stand side by side,
Against all doubt's whispers, together we bide.

Through trials we navigate, hand in hand we tread,
Each step brings us closer to where angels have led.
In the warmth of your gaze, my worries take flight,
Trust is the anchor that holds us so tight.

With hearts open wide, we let love bestow,
A garden of courage that continues to grow.
The light of our bond illuminates the night,
In the tapestry of life, love reigns as our right.

When storms threaten peace, we weather the fight,
The light of trust shines stronger, setting wrongs right.
In laughter and silence, our souls intertwine,
Against all doubt, this love is divine.

So let us remember, as years come and go,
The light of our trust is a treasure to show.
In the depths of the dark, we will never lose sight,
For our hearts beat as one in the warmth of the light.

Unseen Ties of a Devout Affection

In silence prayers weave, so tender and true,
Hearts entwined by faith, in all that we do.
Each whisper of grace, a bond ever strong,
Guided by the light, we know we belong.

Through valleys of doubt, we walk hand in hand,
Together we stand, forever we'll band.
With love like a river, flow gently and wise,
In the arms of the divine, we rise to the skies.

In the shadow of trials, our spirits ignite,
Embraced by His love, we shine through the night.
Every challenge we face, a lesson to learn,
As faith's gentle fire in our hearts starts to burn.

With gratitude's song, we lift our hearts high,
In the warmth of His love, like the stars in the sky.
We cherish each moment, both laughter and tears,
For the unseen ties grow stronger through years.

In the gaze of the divine, our souls intertwine,
Boundless affection, a love so divine.
Together in spirit, no distance can sever,
Through life's sacred journey, we are blessed forever.

Graceful Bonds Amidst Life's Trials

When storms rage around, and shadows appear,
In unity's embrace, we conquer our fear.
Each struggle a thread, in the fabric we weave,
With faith as our anchor, we never deceive.

Through valleys of doubt, and mountains we climb,
Love's gentle whisper cuts through every grime.
In moments of darkness, His light we will find,
As hearts gather close, in the sacred aligned.

Held tight by His grace, we rise through the strife,
Together we flourish, this beautiful life.
In trials and triumphs, our spirits dance free,
Bound by devotion, forever we'll be.

In every kind word, and every shared glance,
We find in each other a sacred romance.
Our hands woven strong, through the toughest of weather,
At the heart of our bond, lies a love that won't tether.

As seasons keep changing, our roots run so deep,
In love's gentle cradle, we sow what we reap.
With each passing moment, grace guides our way,
In the tapestry of life, we choose to stay.

Radiant Journeys in Love's Embrace

With each step we take, in life's winding road,
Love guides us forward, lightening our load.
In the warmth of each smile, and the touch of a hand,
We cherish the moments, together we stand.

Each heartbeat a testament, a promise we share,
In the depth of our souls, a love beyond compare.
Through laughter and tears, our journeys align,
In love's sacred dance, our spirits entwine.

Together we wander through meadows and skies,
In the beauty of nature, true love never lies.
With faith as our compass, we roam ever wide,
In the arms of the heavens, we joyfully glide.

As the dawn breaks anew, with colors so bright,
Our hearts sing a chorus, a symphony of light.
In the radiance of love, every fear fades away,
With every shared dream, we embrace a new day.

In moments of silence, our souls softly speak,
Finding beauty in peace, it's the warmth that we seek.
With gratitude whispered, beneath starlit skies,
In the dance of creation, our love ever flies.

Through the ebb and the flow, we journey as one,
In the embrace of love, life's battles are won.
With every sunrise, our destinies blend,
In the sacred adventure, our hearts will transcend.

Shadows Turned Gold in Holy Light

In whispers of dusk, when the world's set to rest,
We seek in His light, our spirits are blessed.
In shadows that linger, His warmth will ignite,
Transforming our fears into hope shining bright.

Each tear that we shed, becomes part of our grace,
In the journey of faith, we find our true place.
With love as our guide, through the dark we will roam,
In the arms of the Savior, we find our true home.

With every soft prayer, our hearts start to soar,
Revealing the path to what we should implore.
In the quiet of night, when the world feels so cold,
We gather together, turning shadows to gold.

In the tapestry woven, each thread speaks of love,
As we lift our voices to praises above.
Through valleys of doubt, He leads us with care,
In the glow of His truth, we find joy to share.

United in spirit, our burdens grow light,
In the depths of our hearts, His love takes its flight.
With faith as our shield, we walk through the fray,
For every shadow, His light will display.

So let us rejoice, in the blessings we hold,
With hearts intertwined, our story unfolds.
In the promise of dawn, as we rise from the night,
We're shadows turned gold, in the warmth of His light.

Milton Keynes UK
Ingram Content Group UK Ltd.
UKHW020040271124
451585UK00012B/972